The Christmas Book

By Susan Baker

GROSSET & DUNLAP
A FILMWAYS COMPANY
Publishers • New York

Cover illustration
Fiona French

Illustrators
Frank Baber
pages 4-5, 8-9, 12-13, 16-17,
26-27, 36-37, 44-45
Kim Blundell
pages 14, 15, 20-21, 22-23,
30-31, 34-35, 38, 39, 40-41,
46-47
Sara Cole
pages 6-7, 10-11, 18, 19,
24-25, 28-29, 32-33, 42-43

Fiction
page 16, The First Christmas
ⓒ Richard Blythe 1978
page 39, A Christmas King in a
Paper Crown ⓒ Richard Blythe 1978
page 46, The Brothers of
Bethlehem ⓒ Richard Blythe 1978

Advisory panel
Margot Lindsay, librarian
Margaret Payne, teacher

First published 1978
Macdonald Educational Ltd

ⓒ Macdonald Educational Ltd 1978

First U.S. printing 1979
All rights reserved.
Published simultaneously in Canada.
Published in the United States
by Grosset & Dunlap, Inc.

ISBN: 0-448-16563-5 (Trade Edition)
ISBN: 0-448-13612-0 (Library Edition)

Library of Congress Catalog Card No. 79-51212

Printed in the United States of America.

Contents

The First Santa Claus

Christmas is the time of year when we celebrate the birthday of Christ. The church is lit with candles for the Christmas service. Carol singers go from house to house. People kiss under the mistletoe and shake hands as a sign of friendship. We hang up evergreens in our houses and decorate trees with glittering ornaments and lights. We have a special Christmas dinner. Children in many places dress up in paper hats and play games. And most exciting of all, we give presents, just as the shepherds and kings gave presents to the new-born child in Bethlehem, nearly two thousand years ago.

Dutch children do not have to wait until Christmas Day for all their presents. On December 6, which is St Nicholas' Day, they are visited by a kind old gentleman with a long white beard. He is dressed like a bishop in a long red cape with a mitre on his head and a crook in his hand. He comes from Spain in a sailing ship. Crowds of children dress up in their national costumes and greet him in Amsterdam.

St Nicholas rides on a white horse to visit each house where he asks the parents if their children have been good. One of his attendants writes down the answer in a book. That night, the children fill their wooden clogs or shoes with carrots for his horse. They put them beside the big kitchen stove, or on the window sill. Next morning, good children find the carrots gone and their shoes filled with candy and little presents. Very naughty children find only a bunch of sticks.

The first St Nicholas was a bishop over a thousand years ago. He once saved the lives of some children, and he was a very good man, so he became the patron saint of all children.

St Nicholas visits children in other countries too. When the Dutch settlers went to America three hundred years ago they spread the tradition of their St Nicholas, or Santa Klaus as they called him. That is how we get the name Santa Claus. In America, his white horse disappeared and he now rides in a sleigh pulled by reindeer.

Advent Calendar

During the month before Christmas everyone is busy getting everything ready. The traditional time for making cakes and puddings was Stir-Up Sunday at the end of November. Next comes Advent Sunday. In Germany they hang up Advent wreaths of holly with four red candles in the center. They light one candle each Sunday and the last on Christmas Eve. Children count the days until Christmas using an Advent calendar. They open one window each day and find a Christmas picture inside. Why not make one of your own!

You will need
brush
paints
scissors
paper
card
crayons
pencil
glue
old cards, scraps, stamps or seals

1. Draw a picture on cardboard with 23 little windows and one big one.

2. Paint the picture. Number each window. Let the paint dry.

3. Collect little pictures to fit inside each window. Use scraps cut from old cards, stamps, seals — or draw your own pictures.

4. Paste the pictures inside the windows. The last big window is usually a nativity scene.

5. Cut some small squares of paper to fit over the windows like shutters. Glue them on at one side.

6. Use crayons to color in the window covers when the glue is dry.

Start using your calendar on December 1st. Open one window each day.

Our calendar shows the children in this house getting ready for Christmas. They are keeping Christmas traditions from many countries, so they have something different to do every day.

Here are some other suggestions for calendar pictures – a village, a ship, a Christmas tree.

Evergreens

Many of our Christmas customs began thousands of years before Christ was born, when people worshipped the Sun. The Sun gave them heat and light which they needed to stay alive. Every winter the days get shorter until mid December, when they begin to lengthen again. This was the time for a celebration when the people could look forward to the end of winter and the coming of spring. In northern countries the festival was called Yule. It was a time for feasting, singing, dancing and other noisy entertainments.

Evergreens, which are plants that keep their leaves and even produce flowers and fruit, throughout the winter, seemed magical to these people. In northern countries, when they cleaned their houses for the winter festival, they took sweet-smelling pine branches, rosemary and other evergreens into the houses to lay on the damp floors and decorate the walls.

Most important of all was the yule log, the biggest log that could be found, perhaps a whole tree root. This was dragged home in a procession and laid in the huge open fireplace to give heat and light during the festival. It would be lit on Christmas Eve and kept burning for days. Some people kept a piece of each year's log and put it on the fire the following year.

Nowadays, the most important decoration is the Christmas tree. Queen Victoria's husband Prince Albert brought the first Christmas tree to Windsor Castle in 1834 for the royal family. Many other families in England soon copied this German tradition.

All these plants are traditional evergreens, except Poinsettia which is now a popular indoor plant at Christmas.

Christmas rose

bay laurel

ivy

yew

rosemary

mistletoe

pine

Poinsettia

holly

Christmas Cards

Christmas cards became popular just over a hundred years ago. The first ones were decorated with flowers and looked rather like birthday cards. Christmas scenes with robins, holly, snow scenes and people dressed in their best winter clothes came later. Nativity scenes, angels and other religious pictures also became popular. We still send cards like these, as well as modern designs.

Some cards were very elaborate, with pop-up pictures and moving parts. Here are two ways of making some extra special Christmas cards.

A Christmas Piece.
Children copied out prayers or wrote Christmas greetings to their parents on pieces of decorated card.

Pop-up card. You will need

ruler
crayons   glue
scissors
stiff paper

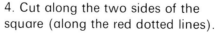

1. Cut two pieces of paper about 8 in. by 12 in. Fold them in half, then open them out flat.

2. Inside one piece, draw a square in the middle about 4 in. by 4 in.

The Three Kings will pop up

3. Draw a picture on it with the part you want to pop up inside the square.

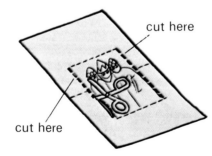

cut here

cut here

4. Cut along the two sides of the square (along the red dotted lines).

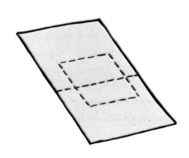

cut here

do not cut he

5. Cut along the top of your pop-up, but do not cut the 'shoulders' at the sides.

crease and fold

6. Crease and fold forwards along the top and bottom of the square (along the blue dotted lines).

crease and fold

7. Crease the shoulders (blue dotted lines) and fold them backwards.

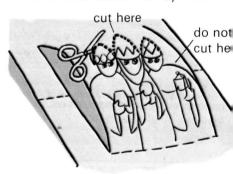

glue at edge only

8. Use glue at the edges to stick the pop-up inside the second piece of folded paper.

10

Victorian Christmas cards

This was one of the very first Christmas cards, designed in 1843

Pictures of the Christmas mail coach are still popular

The Victorians were fond of sad pictures of robins which reminded them of the cold and hungry.

Bell card. You will need
pieces of cardboard

card   crayons

glue

ruler

scissors   paper fastener

1. Draw a bell 2 in. high on cardboard. Color it and cut it out.

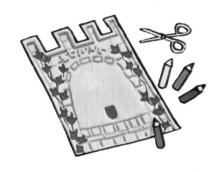

2. Draw a background for the bell on piece of cardboard 4 in. by 4 in. Color it. Write a Christmas message.

3. Attach top of the bell to the background card with a paper fastener.

lever

4. Cut a narrow strip of stiff cardboard 4 in. long to make a lever. Color one end to look like a bell rope.

slit

5. Make a slit across the background card behind the bell.

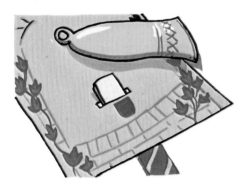

6. Push the plain end of the lever through the slit from behind the card.

7. Hold lever and bell straight. Lift the bell and glue tip of lever to back of bell.

8. When glue is dry, move 'rope' lever gently from side to side to make bell swing.

Carol Singers

Christmas is a time for visiting friends and relations, settling quarrels and giving presents.

In many countries children walk from house to house singing carols and wishing everybody a happy Christmas. Curtains are not drawn so that the light from the windows is a welcoming sign to travellers and visitors.

In Mexico people dress up and go in procession to visit each house in memory of Mary and Joseph's search for a place to stay in Bethlehem.

In Germany and Austria the children go around on the Thursday before Christmas making a lot of noise with bells, whistles and drums. Some of them dress up in ugly masks and chase people. This is because of the old superstition that the dark winter nights are haunted by evil goblins, ghosts and trolls. The noise and the masks are supposed to frighten evil spirits away.

On Christmas Eve the church bells ring for the midnight service. In the snowy mountain villages there are beautiful strings of flickering lights all over the mountainsides as people make their way to church by torchlight.

On the eve of January 6 children dress up as the Three Kings and carry a star round the houses, singing carols. There are Star Singers in many European countries.

In England, the carol singers used to be called wassail singers because their cry of greeting was 'wassail' meaning 'be whole' or 'good health'. They would be invited into each house and given cakes or mince pies and a warm drink from the wassail bowl. One type of drink was called lambswool. It was made from spiced ale with roasted apples.

Carol singers nowadays usually collect money to give away to a charity. But in the days when many people worked on farms, there was no work in the middle of winter and their families were often cold and hungry. Wassailing rich people was a way of getting some warm food and drink and wishing their masters good health at the same time. In one part of Germany the singers pushed a pitchfork through the doorway, expecting food to be stuck on the prongs for them to take away.

Christmas Carols

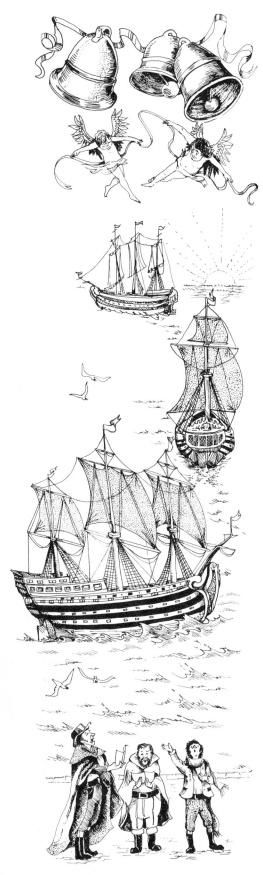

I Saw Three Ships

The old carol I Saw Three Ships has a lot of verses with many of the same lines repeated. There is only one new line of words to learn for each verse. The lively tune is easy to sing and has a good rhythm. Carols like this began as 'round songs' for people to sing while they were doing a 'round dance.' About eight people formed a circle and danced round in a complicated pattern.

Many carols began as popular songs. Singing and dancing were all part of the fun of Christmas. That is why so many old carols have such lively tunes.

To sing I Saw Three Ships as a round song, form into two groups of singers. Group 1 sings verses 1, 3, 5 and 7. Group 2 sings verses 2, 4, 6 and 8. All sing verse 9.

I saw three ships come sail - ing in,
On Christ - mas Day, on Christ - mas Day,
I saw three ships come sail - ing in,
On Christ - mas Day in the morn - ing.

Verse 2 And what was in those ships all three?
On Christmas Day, on Christmas Day,
And what was in those ships all three?
On Christmas Day in the morning.

Verse 3 Our Saviour Christ and His Lady.

Verse 4 Pray, whither sailed those ships all three?

Verse 5 Oh, they sailed into Bethlehem.

Verse 6 And all the bells on earth shall ring.

Verse 7 And all the angels in Heav'n shall sing.

Verse 8 And all the souls on earth shall sing.

Verse 9 Then let us all rejoice. Amen.

Silent Night

Silent Night was first sung in 1818, in the village church at Oberndorf, near Salzburg in Austria. There is a story telling how Christmas was almost spoiled for the villagers that year.

On Christmas Eve, the priest went into the church and found that the organ would not work. The leather bellows, which are used to pump the air through the organ pipes, were full of holes. They had been nibbled by hungry mice! Christmas without music would be terrible! So the priest showed the organist Franz Bauer a new Christmas hymn he had written. Franz quickly composed a tune for it which could be played on a guitar. So Oberndorf had music after all.

Si - lent night, ho - ly night.

All is calm, all is bright

Round yon Vir - gin Mo - ther and Child.

Ho - ly In - fant so ten - der and mild,

Sleep in heav - en - ly peace,

Sleep in heav - en - ly peace.

Verse 2

Silent night, holy night!
Shepherds first saw the light,
Heard resounding clear and long,
Far and near, the angel song:
Christ the Saviour is here,
Christ the Saviour is here.

Verse 3

Silent night, holy night!
Son of God, oh how bright,
Love is smiling from Thy face!
Peals for us the hour of grace.
Christ our Saviour is born,
Christ our Saviour is born.

The First Christmas

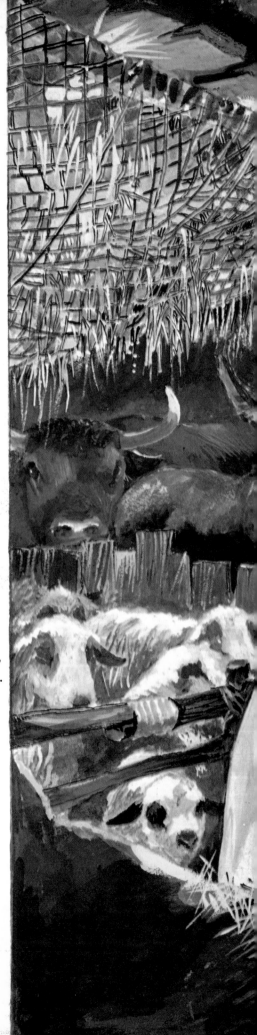

Once upon a time, nearly two thousand years ago, a carpenter named Joseph made a difficult journey. The ruler of Rome said that all the people of his empire must be taxed, so Joseph and his wife went to a town where the tax-gatherers could write down their names.

It was the coldest time of winter. Joseph walked all the way, and his wife, who was called Mary, rode on their donkey. Mary was going to have a baby, so Joseph had to take great care of her.

When they arrived at the town, which was called Bethlehem, Mary and Joseph found that every inn was already full. Mary knew her baby was to be born very soon, but there was nowhere for them to go. The only place where they might shelter was a stable.

That same night, on a hill near Bethlehem, some shepherds were keeping guard over their sheep when a strange and wonderful thing happened. It seemed as if all the cold hillside suddenly blazed with light. The Shepherds did not know it, but at that moment, in Bethlehem, Mary's baby was born.

The shepherds were frightened. The light around them grew brighter. Their ears were filled with sound, as if the stars themselves were singing. Each fell to his knees, certain that all that blaze and brilliance must come from God. They seemed to hear voices in the light, telling them to go to Bethlehem to find a new-born king.

In the icy darkness, they stumbled down the hill, dazed and scarcely knowing where they went. They reached Bethlehem just before dawn. All was cold and silent, but they saw a light, a lantern, shining in a stable. They went, and looked inside.

Joseph and Mary were kneeling there, beside a cattle-manger where a baby lay, warmly wrapped.

Joseph beckoned. 'This is the Prince of Heaven,' he said, 'sent to us to comfort men and guide them to God.'

Mary's eyes glistened with tears. She stroked the cheek of the sleeping child, saying,

'This is my dear son. His name is Jesus.'

All the stable seemed to glow with light, and on that first Christmas morning the shepherds, too, knelt before Mary's son and bowed down in wonder.

by Richard Blythe

Christmas Crib

You will need

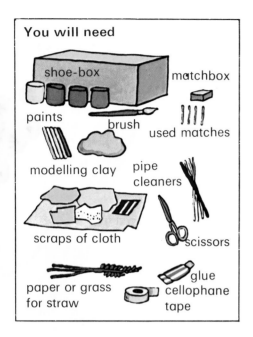

shoe-box
matchbox
paints
brush
used matches
modelling clay
pipe cleaners
scraps of cloth
scissors
paper or grass for straw
glue
cellophane tape

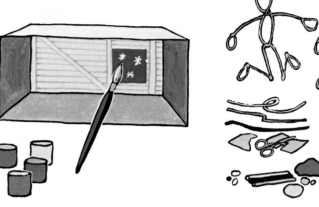

1. Paint a shoebox to look like the stable.

2. Make people from pipe cleaners or modeling clay. Dress them in cloth scraps.

3. Make animals from pipe cleaners or clay.

4. Make manger from matchbox. Cut it in half to make a trough. Attach match legs.

In Spanish and Italian homes the crib is the most important part of the Christmas decorations.

5. Put grass or shredded paper in manger and on floor as straw. Arrange figures around crib.

What Did Santa Claus Bring?

Pat and Jan are dreaming about all the things that Santa might bring. There are fourteen different Christmas surprises hidden in the picture. Can you find them all? If you could choose just one of these presents, which one would it be?

Christmas Presents

Father Christmas

La Befana

Christkindl

Giving presents is a way of showing people that you like them. Long ago people used to give each other presents of candles and dolls during the winter festival. Now we give presents as a reminder of the Christmas message. 'Peace on earth and good will to all men'.

The most exciting presents are the children's toys.

In England, Father Christmas delivers them during the night before Christmas. The children leave an empty stocking or pillowcase hanging at the end of the bed. In the morning they hope it will be full of presents.

In Germany the traditional visitor is the Christkindl who is the Christ Child's messenger. She is a beautiful fair-haired girl with a shining crown of candles who visits each house with a basket of presents. In some German homes a room is locked up before Christmas. On Christmas Eve the children go to bed but are woken up at midnight by their parents and taken down to the locked room. The door is opened and they see the tree all lit up, with piles of parcels on little tables.

In Scandinavia a little gnome called Julenisse puts the presents under the Christmas tree in the night. The children leave a bowl of porridge out for him. In Russia someone called Grandfather Frost brings children presents in December.

In Spain and Italy the children wait until Epiphany, January 6, for their presents. In Spain they are brought by the Three Kings on their camels. The children go out in the evening to look for them but no one has ever managed to catch sight of them. So they put their shoes on the window sill or balcony, with some straw for the camels, before they go to bed. Next morning they find presents there, just like the Dutch children do after a visit from St Nicholas.

La Befana, the kind witch, brings the presents to Italian children on January 6. She was a woman who followed the wise men but got lost. She has been wandering Italy ever since, giving presents to children at Christmas.

On the day after Christmas people give tradesmen money. In England this is called Boxing Day because boys used to go round collecting money in clay boxes. When the boxes were full, they broke them open.

Julenisse

Grandfather Frost

The Three Kings

St Nicholas

A Visit from Saint Nicholas

'Twas the night before Christmas, when all through the house
Not a creature was stirring, not even a mouse;
The stockings were hung by the chimney with care,
In hopes that Saint Nicholas soon would be there;
The children were nestled all snug in their beds,
While visions of sugar-plums danced in their heads;
And Mamma in her 'kerchief, and I in my cap,
Had just settled our brains for a long winter's nap,
When out on the lawn there arose such a clatter,
I sprang from the bed to see what was the matter.

Away to the window I flew like a flash,
Tore open the shutters and threw up the sash.
The moon on the breast of the new-fallen snow
Gave the lustre of mid-day to objects below,
When, what to my wondering eyes should appear,
But a miniature sleigh, and eight tiny reindeer,
With a little old driver, so lively and quick,
I knew in a moment it must be Saint Nick.

More rapid than eagles his coursers they came,
And he whistled, and shouted, and called them by name;
'Now, *Dasher*! Now, *Dancer*! Now *Prancer* and *Vixen*!
On, *Comet!* On, *Cupid!* On, *Donner* and *Blitzen!*
To the top of the porch! To the top of the wall!
Now dash away! Dash away! Dash away all!'
As dry leaves that before the wild hurricane fly,
When they meet with an obstacle, mount to the sky;
So up to the house-top the coursers they flew,
With the sleigh full of toys, and Saint Nicholas too.

by Clement Clarke Moore

And then, in a twinkling, I heard on the roof
The prancing and pawing of each little hoof.
As I drew in my head, and was turning around,
Down the chimney Saint Nicholas came with a bound.
He was dressed all in fur, from his head to his foot,
And his clothes were all tarnished with ashes and soot;
A bundle of toys he had flung on his back,
And he looked like a pedlar just opening his pack.

His eyes – how they twinkled! His dimples how merry!
His cheeks were like roses, his nose like a cherry!
His droll little mouth was drawn up like a bow,
And the beard of his chin was as white as the snow;
The stump of a pipe he held tight in his teeth,
And the smoke it encircled his head like a wreath;
He had a broad face and a little round belly,
That shook when he laughed, like a bowl full of jelly.
He was chubby and plump, a right jolly old elf,
And I laughed when I saw him, in spite of myself;
A wink of his eye and twist of his head,
Soon gave me to know I had nothing to dread.

He spoke not a word, but went straight to his work,
And filled all the stockings; then turned with a jerk,
And laying his finger aside of his nose,
And giving a nod, up the chimney he rose;
He sprang to his sleigh, to his team gave a whistle,
And away they all flew like the down of a thistle.
But I heard him exclaim, ere he drove out of sight,
'Happy Christmas to all, and to all a good-night'.

Christmas Decorations

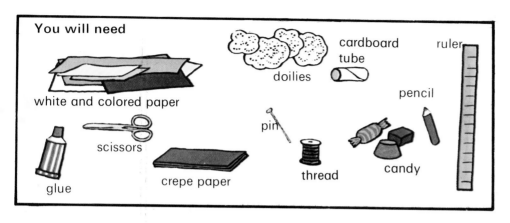

You will need

white and colored paper · doilies · cardboard tube · ruler · pencil · scissors · glue · crepe paper · pin · thread · candy

Twisted Chains

1. Cut a long paper strip 2 in. wide from a roll of crepe paper.

2. Fold strip in accordion pleats. Cut pattern around edge.

3. Unfold it. Twist it around and around. Fasten it up at the ends.

Ring Chains

1. Cut 20 strips of colored paper 1 in. wide and 6 in. long.

2. Make one ring. Glue ends.

3. Slip next strip through. Make ring. Glue ends. Use up all the strips like this.

Folded Chains

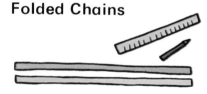

1. Cut two long narrow strips of paper $\frac{3}{4}$ in. wide.

2. Lay ends together. Fold strips over each other in turn as in A, B, C and D.

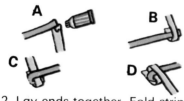

3. Glue on more strips to make chain longer. Glue down last end.

Party Snappers

1. Fill cardboard tube with candy. Roll up in paper.

2. Glue edge and tie ends with thread.

3. Trim ends and fan out.

Heart Baskets

1. Cut these shapes out of two folded bits of paper. Cut slits across the folds.

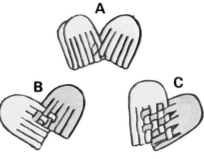

2. Weave the two together as in A, B and C.

3. Open heart-shaped basket. Attach handle. Hang up.

Snowflakes

1. Cut circle of white paper. Trim around edge.

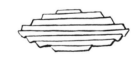

2. Fold in accordion pleats.

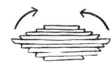

3. Pull ends together and glue.

4. Make another one the same way. Glue sides together. Hang up with thread.

5. Glue 3 together to make a 6-pointed star.

6. Doilies may be used, too.

Fasting and Feasting

Roast turkey, plum pudding, mince pies and Christmas cake make an enormous meal. Not so very long ago, many people did not get enough to eat during most of the winter. By December, most of the store of hay and corn would be used up and the animals which had lived on it had to be slaughtered. Then people could look forward to a feast at Christmas.

In many countries people kept pigs which were fattened up for Christmas. The boar's head was served with an apple in its mouth and a garland of rosemary. Some people roasted a whole pig on a spit. Others had just a joint of pork or a cured ham. In Austria, pork was made into special sausages.

Everywhere, people tried to give themselves a treat and have something special to eat. Roast goose was popular in England, but now most people have roast turkey. Peacock used to be served, with all its feathers put back over it after it was cooked. In Scandinavia they eat roasted pork ribs, salted cod and a special rice

pudding. In countries a long way from the sea, fish is a special treat and is the main dish at Christmas.

In England, Christmas dinner was usually eaten at midday on December 25, during daylight. In Spain, families had their meal immediately after Midnight Mass on Christmas Eve. In Finland the meal was begun as soon as the first star appeared in the sky.

In every country it was usual to fast, or starve, before the feast. In England, the only thing that people ate on the day before the feast was frumenty, a kind of porridge made from corn. Over the years the recipe changed. Eggs, fruit, spices, lumps of meat and dried plums were added. The whole mixture was wrapped in a cloth and boiled. This is how plum pudding began. Nowadays more fruit is put in instead of meat. Mince pies also contained meat.

Christmas feasts have always included nuts, fruit, candy, cakes and cookies. Gingerbread men and animals are popular gifts in many countries.

Christmas Cakes and Cookies

St Nicholas Letters

Dutch children are given St Nicholas Letter cookies on December 6th.

You will need

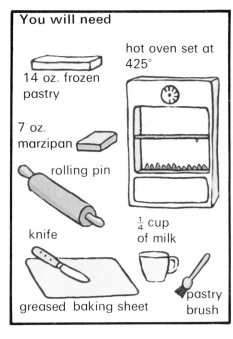

14 oz. frozen pastry

hot oven set at 425°

7 oz. marzipan

rolling pin

knife

$\frac{1}{4}$ cup of milk

greased baking sheet

pastry brush

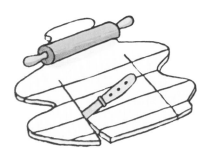

1. Thaw pastry. Roll it out thinly on floured surface. Cut it into strips about 4 in. by $1\frac{3}{4}$ in.

2. Roll marzipan into 'worms' 4 in. long and as thin as your finger.

3. Roll marzipan worms up in the strips of pastry. Dab milk on edges and ends and press to seal them.

4. Shape each pastry roll into a letter. Try IOUSLCPSZ and V first. Seal joins with milk.

5. Use strips of different lengths to make up other letters. Space letters out on a greased baking tray. Brush tops with milk.

6. Bake for 10-15 minutes in oven. Ask a grown-up to help take them out. Let them cool before tasting.

Chocolate Log

In France the traditional Christmas cake is a chocolate log. Here is a way to make an uncooked one.

1. Put the cream, sugar and cocoa in a basin. Beat cream until it is just stiff enough to stand in peaks.

2. Spread the cream on the cookies. Sandwich them together in a long roll. Use about half the cream.

3. Wrap the roll of cookies in foil. Put it in refrigerator with the rest of the cream.

4. Next day, unwrap the roll, put it on a plate and cover it with the rest of the cream.

5. Drag a fork over the cream to make 'bark' on the 'log'. Decorate it with sugar snow and holly.

6. This cake is rich, so serve small slices. Eat it with a fork or spoon. Slices cut at an angle look best.

Christmas in the Sun

Christmas makes people think of snow, reindeer and roast turkey, even if they live in Africa or Australia, where it is hot in December because it is summer.

The shop windows are decorated with artificial snow while people do their Christmas shopping wearing light summer clothes.

There are street carnivals with Santa Claus on his sleigh pulled by reindeer, though it is not wintry weather. Santa must feel quite uncomfortable, dressed up in a red suit trimmed with fur.

In Mexico there are torchlight processions after dark during the weeks before Christmas. On Christmas Eve there are fireworks as well.

In these countries all the summer flowers can be used in the decorations.

In Australia it is warm enough to sit out of doors at night. Hundreds of people gather in the parks in the big cities and sing carols by candlelight.

Santa on a surfboard

A Christmas street carnival on a sunny summer's day

The great feast, which is now a traditional Christmas dinner with roast turkey, plum pudding and mince pies, is the kind of meal for people to eat in winter, not on a hot summer's day. But they do!

In very hot countries they wait until the cool of the evening to serve food on porches of their bungalows and eat by candlelight.

Many people eat Christmas dinner out of doors. In Australia, some families picnic in the garden, the country, or on the beach. They often take a whole meal with them, not just turkey sandwiches. They may even bring along a small tree, complete with decorations.

Santa Claus visits some of these parties. He has all sorts of different ways of travelling. In Singapore he sails in on a catamaran. In California he rides a surfboard. He is rowed up to Bondi Beach in Australia in a surfboat. He has even been seen on water skis and in a coach pulled by emus.

Christmas dinner on the beach

A Mexican Christmas Eve procession with fireworks and flaming torches

Reindeer Race

Every year, Santa Claus chooses a team of reindeer to draw his sleigh. There is always a tremendous race to be the first to reach him.

Play the Reindeer Race game with your friends. You will need a die and some counters or buttons. You can make the game very exciting by using two counters each. The first person to get his counters to Santa is the winner.

Choose between north and south when you get to the middle. Throw the exact number to finish.

Swim across lake. Move on 5 in direction of arrow.

Slip on ice trying to take short cut. Miss a turn.

You forgot to polish your antlers. Go back 3.

Stop to eat. Miss a turn.

START

Hear someone coming. Hurry on 6 places.

Antlers get tangled in trees Go back 6.

The mountain path is stony and slippery. Go back 1.

Follow the arrow along short cut through forest.

Lost in forest. Follow arrow and go round again.

Stop to r before mountai Miss a tu

Practice flying.
Move on 3.

Fall in
snowdrift.
Go back 6.

Catch a cold.
Miss a turn.

Chased by angry
polar bears.
Escape by following
arrow.

Choose
between
going North
or South.

N
S

Get
sunburned.
Go back 2.

Have a race with
kangaroos. Move
on 3.

FINISH

Go to a
beach party.
Miss a turn.

Join a street
carnival
Follow the arrow.

Give koala bear a
ride. Move on 6.

Help fruit farmer who
shows you short cut.
Follow the arrow.

Bob Cratchit's Christmas

This story about a Victorian family's Christmas Day comes from the famous book A Christmas Carol by Charles Dickens. Bob Cratchit was a poor clerk who worked for a mean old man called Ebenezer Scrooge who hated Christmas. One Christmas Eve, Scrooge was haunted by ghosts who showed him what awful things would happen if he went on being mean and miserable at Christmas.

In this part of the story, the Ghost of Christmas Present is showing Scrooge Bob Cratchit's home.

They are not a rich family. There are six children and one of them is a cripple. Their clothes are shabby and there is not a lot to eat—but they are much happier than old Scrooge.

Mrs Cratchit, dressed but poorly in a twice-turned gown, laid the cloth, assisted by Belinda Cratchit, second of her daughters; while Master Peter Cratchit plunged a fork into the saucepan of potatoes, getting the corners of his monstrous shirt collar into his mouth. And now two smaller Cratchits, boy and girl, came tearing in, screaming that outside the baker's they had smelt the goose, and known it for their own; and basking in luxurious thoughts of sage and onion, these young Cratchits danced about the table. Master Peter Cratchit (although his collars nearly choked him) blew the fire, until the slow potatoes bubbling up, knocked loudly at the saucepan lid to be let out and peeled.

'What has ever got your father then?' said Mrs Cratchit. 'And your brother, Tiny Tim! And Martha warn't as late last Christmas Day by half-an-hour!'

'Here's Martha, Mother!' said a girl, appearing as she spoke.

'Here's Martha!' cried the two young Cratchits. 'Hurrah! There's *such* a goose, Martha!'

'Why, bless your heart alive, my dear, how late you are!' said Mrs Cratchit, kissing her a dozen times, and taking off her shawl and bonnet for her.

'We'd a deal of work to finish up last night,' replied the girl, 'and had to clear away this morning, Mother!'

'Well! Never mind so long as you are come,' said Mrs Cratchit. 'Sit ye down before the fire, my dear, and have a warm, Lord bless ye!'

'No, no! There's Father coming!' cried the two young Cratchits, who were everywhere at once. 'Hide, Martha, hide!'

So Martha hid herself, and in came Bob, the father, his threadbare clothes darned and brushed, to look seasonable; and Tiny Tim upon his shoulder. Alas for Tiny Tim, he bore a little crutch, and had his limbs supported by an iron frame!

'Why, where's our Martha?' cried Bob Cratchit, looking round.

'Not coming,' said Mrs Cratchit.

'Not coming!' said Bob. 'Not coming upon Christmas Day!'

Martha didn't like to see him disappointed, so she came out from behind the door, and ran into his arms, while the two young Cratchits hustled Tiny Tim, and bore him off into the wash-house, that he might hear the pudding singing in the copper.

'And how did little Tim behave?' asked Mrs Cratchit, when Bob had hugged his daughter to his heart's content.

'As good as gold,' said Bob, 'and better. Somehow he gets thoughtful, sitting by himself so much, and thinks the strangest things you ever heard. He told me, coming home, that he hoped the people saw him in the church, because he was a cripple, and it might be pleasant to them to remember upon Christmas Day, who made lame beggars walk and blind men see.

His active little crutch was heard upon the floor, and back came Tiny Tim before another word was spoken, escorted by his brother and sister to his stool before the fire; and while Bob, turning up his cuffs—as if, poor fellow, they were capable of being made more shabby—compounded some hot mixture in a jug with gin and lemons, and stirred it round and round and put it on the hob to simmer. Master Peter and the two young Cratchits went to fetch the goose.

Such a bustle ensued that you might have thought a goose the rarest of all birds; and in truth it was something very like it in that house. Mrs Cratchit made the gravy hissing hot; Master Peter mashed the potatoes with incredible vigour; Miss Belinda sweetened up the apple sauce; Martha dusted the hot plates; Bob took Tiny Tim beside him in a tiny corner at the table; the two young Cratchits set chairs for

from A Christmas Carol by Charles Dickens

everybody, not forgetting themselves, and mounting guard upon their posts, crammed spoons into their mouths, lest they should shriek for goose before their turn came to be helped. At last the dishes were set on, and grace was said. It was succeeded by a breathless pause, as Mrs Cratchit, looking slowly all along the carving-knife, prepared to plunge it in the breast; but when she did, and when the long-expected gush of stuffing issued forth, one murmur of delight arose all round the board, and even Tiny Tim, excited by the two young Cratchits, beat on the table with the handle of his knife, and feebly cried Hurrah!

There never was such a goose. Bob said he didn't believe there ever was such a goose cooked. Its tenderness and flavour, size and cheapness, were the themes of universal admiration. Eked out by the apple sauce and mashed potatoes, it was a sufficient dinner for the whole family; indeed, as Mrs Cratchit said with great delight (surveying one small atom of a bone upon the dish), they hadn't ate it all at last! Yet everyone had had enough, and the youngest Cratchits, in particular, were steeped in sage and onion to the eyebrows! But now, the plates being changed by Miss Belinda, Mrs Cratchit left the room alone—too nervous to bear

witnesses—to take the pudding up and bring it in.

Suppose it should not be done enough! Suppose it should break in turning out! Suppose somebody should have got over the wall of the backyard, and stolen it, while they were merry with the goose—a supposition at which the two young Cratchits became livid! All sorts of horrors were supposed.

Halloa! A great deal of steam! The pudding was out of the copper. A smell like a washing-day! That was the cloth. A smell like an eating-house and a pastry-cook's next door to each other, with a laundress's next door to that! That was the pudding! In half a minute Mrs Cratchit entered—flushed, but smiling proudly—with the pudding, like a speckled cannonball, so hard and firm, blazing in ignited brandy, with holly stuck into the top.

Oh, a wonderful pudding! Everybody had something to say about it, but nobody said it was at all a small pudding for a large family. Any Cratchit would have blushed to hint at such a thing.

At last the dinner was all done, the cloth was cleared, the hearth swept, and the fire made up. The compound in the jug being tasted, and considered perfect, apples and oranges were put upon the table, and

a shovelful of chestnuts on the fire. Then all the Cratchit family drew round the hearth in what Bob Cratchit called a circle, meaning half a one; and at Bob Cratchit's elbow stood the family display of glass. Two tumblers, and a custard-cup without a handle.

These held the hot stuff from the jug, however, as well as golden goblets would have done; and Bob served it out with beaming looks, while the chestnuts on the fire sputtered and cracked noisily. Then Bob proposed:

'A Merry Christmas to us all, my dears. God bless us!'

Which all the family re-echoed.

'God bless us every one!' said Tiny Tim, the last of all.

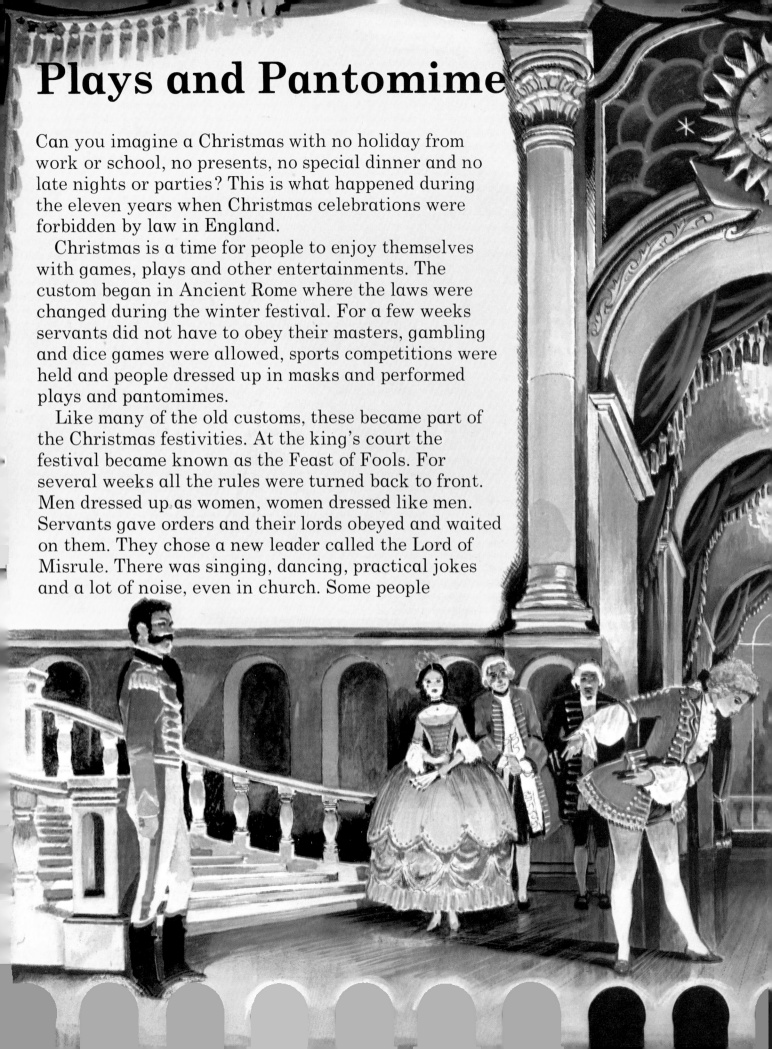

Plays and Pantomime

Can you imagine a Christmas with no holiday from work or school, no presents, no special dinner and no late nights or parties? This is what happened during the eleven years when Christmas celebrations were forbidden by law in England.

Christmas is a time for people to enjoy themselves with games, plays and other entertainments. The custom began in Ancient Rome where the laws were changed during the winter festival. For a few weeks servants did not have to obey their masters, gambling and dice games were allowed, sports competitions were held and people dressed up in masks and performed plays and pantomimes.

Like many of the old customs, these became part of the Christmas festivities. At the king's court the festival became known as the Feast of Fools. For several weeks all the rules were turned back to front. Men dressed up as women, women dressed like men. Servants gave orders and their lords obeyed and waited on them. They chose a new leader called the Lord of Misrule. There was singing, dancing, practical jokes and a lot of noise, even in church. Some people

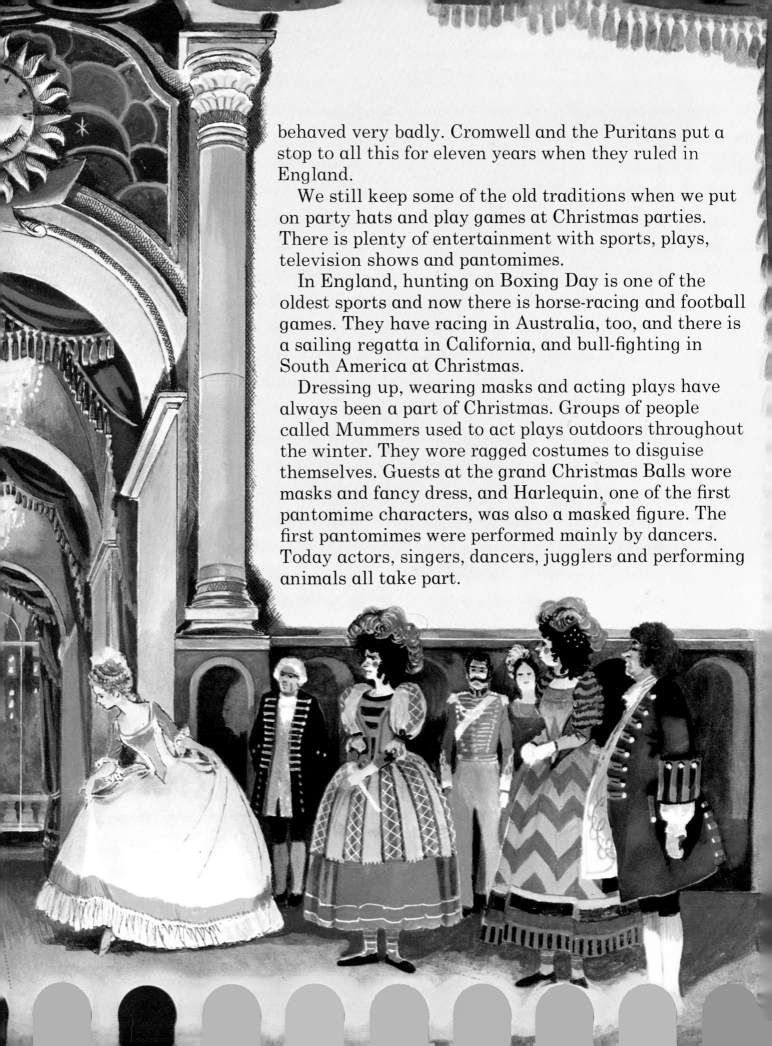

behaved very badly. Cromwell and the Puritans put a stop to all this for eleven years when they ruled in England.

We still keep some of the old traditions when we put on party hats and play games at Christmas parties. There is plenty of entertainment with sports, plays, television shows and pantomimes.

In England, hunting on Boxing Day is one of the oldest sports and now there is horse-racing and football games. They have racing in Australia, too, and there is a sailing regatta in California, and bull-fighting in South America at Christmas.

Dressing up, wearing masks and acting plays have always been a part of Christmas. Groups of people called Mummers used to act plays outdoors throughout the winter. They wore ragged costumes to disguise themselves. Guests at the grand Christmas Balls wore masks and fancy dress, and Harlequin, one of the first pantomime characters, was also a masked figure. The first pantomimes were performed mainly by dancers. Today actors, singers, dancers, jugglers and performing animals all take part.

Pantomime Puzzle

In the theatre the Christmas pantomime still includes many of the old traditions. Pantomime means 'all in mime', that is, acting without any words. The plot of the pantomime is usually a fairy story. There is always a man in it dressed up as an old lady. The hero is always played by a girl, called the principal boy. The hero or heroine usually begins as a poor unlucky person but ends up rich and famous. This way of turning things upside down is all that is left of the Feast of Fools.

Match these people with the words opposite

1. ALADDIN AND HIS MAGIC LAMP
2. SLEEPING BEAUTY
3. JACK AND THE BEANSTALK
4. WOLF FROM LITTLE RED RIDING HOOD
5. UGLY SISTERS FROM CINDERELLA
6. PUSS IN BOOTS
7. HUMPTY DUMPTY

Answers on page 48

A Christmas King in a Paper Crown

by Richard Blythe

At topsy-turvy Christmas-time,
A-many, many years ago,
For twelve short days I ruled the Court
And told my lords what each must do!

They took my greasy apron off,
They put a crown upon my head.
They laid a sceptre in my hand,
And dressed me royally, in red.

They set me on a Christmas throne,
For twice six days to make the law.
'My Lord Misrule,' they greeted me,
Like subjects, kneeling on the floor!

Yes, down they knelt—the King, his Queen,
Their lords and ladies bold and fair.
They made me King of Christmas-time,
And knelt to do me honor there.

At topsy-turvy Christmas-time
They watched me, should I smile or frown.
For servants were the masters then,
And all the Court was upside-down!

I told the King to wait on us,
To carve our meat and pour us wine.
'The Queen,' I said, 'shall dance and sing,
To bring us joy at Christmas-time!'

I told six Earls to play a dance
For cook and groom and serving-maid.
I told three Dukes to brush the hearth
And see our fire was brightly laid.

'Each lord,' I said, 'shall wear a dress.
Their ladies, they must dress as lords.
You servants, wear your masters' clothes,
Their buckled shoes and silver swords!'

At topsy-turvy Christmas-time,
With sceptre, robe and paper crown,
For twelve short days I turned the Court
First inside-out, then upside-down!

39

New Year

Old Father Time brings in the young New Year

New Year is the time to make a fresh start with some good resolutions. Promise yourself that you will do certain things better in the New Year. In many countries it is the time to settle debts. In France and Germany, New Year's Day is a time for visiting, and grown-ups give each other presents.

New Year's Eve is a time for parties. In Austria someone dresses up as an old man called Sylvester. He wears mistletoe in his hair and goes around kissing all the girls. In Germany they play fortune-telling games. Some people sit around the fire telling ghost stories while they wait for the clock to strike midnight. Others drink and sing in the streets. In Switzerland there are bell-ringing competitions. All this noise is supposed to drive away evil spirits.

In some countries farmers go out to the orchards and wassail the fruit trees. They sing and shout and drink their health. Sometimes they fire shots into the branches. This is supposed to wake up the trees and

Wassailing the fruit trees

New Year street celebrations

drive away evil spirits so that they will bear a good crop of fruit next year.

Even if people do not believe in the old superstitions, they enjoy keeping up these traditions.

At midnight church bells are rung all around the world. In Paris, car drivers toot their horns. In harbors, ships' sirens are sounded.

Everybody should say 'Happy New Year' to the people around them, even if they are strangers.

In Scotland, New Year's Eve is called Hogmanay. After midnight young men go first-footing. The custom gets its name because the first person to set foot in a house in the New Year is supposed to bring good luck. The visitor must have dark hair and bring a present with them. A man with red hair, or any woman, would bring bad luck.

Chinese New Year is celebrated on a different day each year. There are colorful street processions, with masks, fireworks and huge paper dragons.

Ringing in the New Year

First-footing at Hogmanay

Chinese New Year celebrations

Party Games

Christmas has always been a time for fun and games. Hundreds of years ago, there were laws forbidding people to gamble or play games with cards or dice for most of the year. But at Christmas these laws were lifted so people gave parties and enjoyed themselves as much as possible for this short time.

People used to dress up, sing, dance, ring bells and let off fireworks. We still put on hats and create lots of noise with whistles, horns, bells and other things.

Here are some traditional games from around the world which you might like to play at your Christmas party.

Capture the Star

In Alaska people play a Christmas game called Capture the Star. They dress up as the Three Kings and their servants and carry a star from house to house, singing carols. Other children dress up as Herod's soldiers and chase after them and try to capture the star.

Round Song

... On the First day of Christmas
   My true love sent to me
   A Partridge in a Pear Tree ...

Singing songs like this was an old Christmas game. People took turns to sing a verse. Each person had to add a new line and remember all that had gone before.

Play this game at your party. Sit in a circle and take turns singing a verse. Make up your own words. Each person must think of a new 'gift' and add it to the list.

See how many verses you can sing before people start forgetting the gifts. When someone makes a mistake, they are 'out'. The last person should get a prize.

Your song might go like this
... On the Third Day of Christmas
My true love sent to me
Three Blind Mice
Two Tiny Turtles
And a Partridge in a Pear Tree! ...

Dutch Pass the Parcel

In the Netherlands they have a special way of wrapping up parcels. They wrap each present in layers and layers of paper with a rhyme or riddle attached to each wrapper. The riddle gives a clue to what is in the parcel and who it is for. Everyone helps to unwrap it and tries to guess the answer.

Why not make up a parcel like this for a game of Pass the Parcel. Any one guessing a riddle should get a prize.

Ask a grown-up to play some music on a piano, record or cassette. Sit in a circle and pass the parcel around. When the music stops, the person holding the parcel must unwrap a layer and guess at the riddle.

Answers on page 48

1. Half of me is a little dog

2. Half of me is your favorite animal

3. Your fingers will bring me to life.

4. I work in a theatre.

Mexican Pinatas

In Mexico, children get lots of surprise parcels at Christmas. They are called pinatas. The parcels are hung up high and the children hit them with sticks to break them open. Some pinatas contain nice surprises such as candy or little presents. But others have nasty surprises in them instead. When they are broken, the children are showered with bits of paper, feathers, beans, or water.

Make some pinatas up for your party. Decorate large paper bags, Half fill each one with a different surprise. Put wrapped candy in one, scraps of paper in another, dried peas in another, and so on. In the biggest one put tiny presents such as paper hats, whistles and tooters. Tie the bags up with string and hang them up around the house, or across a room on a string.

Breaking the pinatas would be a good game to end your party.

Don't forget to tidy up

The Three Kings

January 6 is called the Epiphany. It is a great feast day in Italy, Spain and many other countries. This is the time when the children get presents in memory of the gifts brought to the Christ Child by the Three Kings. These kings were three wise men who followed a star to Bethlehem. Their names were Caspar, Melchior and Balthazar. They brought valuable gifts of gold, myrrh, which was a scented ointment, and frankincense, which was precious oil. In Spain and France the children go out to look for the Kings, taking gifts of hay for the camels. In Germany boys dress up as kings and carry a star through the village, singing carols.

In France and other countries, families served a Three Kings Cake with a bean hidden in it. Whoever found the bean in their slice was made King, or Queen, for the day.

Another name for this day is Twelfth Day. It is the last of the Twelve Days of Christmas which used to be one long holiday. Twelfth Night parties were very noisy. It was the last night of the Feast of Fools before the Lord of Misrule had to give up his crown and become a servant again.

Twelfth Night is the time when all the decorations should be taken down or they will bring bad luck. All the candy decorating the tree can be eaten—if there is any left! In some cities all the old trees are burned on a huge bonfire. Artificial trees are folded up and packed away with their lights and decorations.

gold

frankincense

myrrh

Myrrh and frankincense come from these plants.
Gold was made into jewelry and coins.

The Brothers of Bethlehem

A story to act round your Nativity scene,
with:
King Herod
His Page and Courtiers
The Three Kings
A Roman Officer
The Three Shepherds
Mary and Joseph
Angel choir

(Scene: the Court of King Herod. A drum beats. Herod enters, followed by a Roman Officer. He mounts his throne)

Herod Call the travellers! Call these wise men, these so-called kings.
Officer Call the travellers!

(A Page enters, followed by the Three Kings)

1st King Greetings, great king.
2nd King Greetings to Herod.
3rd King Greetings to Herod, King of Judea.
Herod You are welcome, sirs. And we thank you for the gifts you bring us.
1st King Ah, King Herod, these gifts are for another king.
2nd King A star rose in the east that shall lead us to a new king. We journey to worship him.
3rd King As the prophets foretold, great Herod, the king we seek shall be found in your land.
Herod A king in my land? I am king in Judea. There is no other king but me.
1st King But you have Roman soldiers in your palace, sir.
2nd King And Roman guards outside its walls.
3rd King Is not Caesar of Rome king of this land?
Herod No, sirs! Herod alone is king of Judea!
Officer Gentle sirs, the great Caesar Augustus, Emperor of Rome, is King Herod's master and protector.
Herod Caesar is master of the world. I am his king in this country. But who are you? Where do you come from? Where are you going?
1st King I am king of a far eastern land. I go to find the king who is newly born in Judea.
2nd King I am king of a far western land. I go to find the king of the world.

3rd King I am king of a far southern land. I follow a star that will lead me to the king of all kings.
Herod East, west, south? Is this king you seek a king in the north?
Officer Caesar is king in the north. Beware how you talk of kings in the presence of a Roman officer!
1st King We talk of only what we know.
Herod You talk foolishly! But go in peace. Follow your star and find your king—if you can!
2nd King Herod is good.
3rd King We thank you, Herod.
Herod But, sirs! Listen to me. Return this way on your journey home. If this king of the world, this king of kings, exists I wish to know where to find him.
Officer Return this way and tell us where this new-born king is.
1st King We shall do so.
2nd King Farewell, great Herod.
3rd King We shall return.

(They bow and go. The Roman Officer steps forward)

Herod Follow them, captain. Find this king who has prophets and stars for his messengers.
Officer Sir, these are old men with old men's foolish dreams. There is no king. Let them wander, sir.
Herod Do as I command! I, too, have heard the old prophecies. I shall find this king and I shall slay him. There shall be no king in Judea but me! Go!
Officer Under Caesar there shall be no king but Herod! I will obey and follow them, sir!

(The Roman Officer exits as the curtains close. Then the Three Kings enter from one side of the forestage and the Three Shepherds from the other side)

1st King Greetings, friends!
2nd King Who are you, friends?
3rd King What is the name of this place?
Shep'd 1 We are shepherds, sir.
Shep'd 2 This, sir, is Bethlehem.
1st King Look! The star has stopped. Our journey is over.

Shep'd 3	A star, sir? While we were watching our sheep on the hillside, we, too, saw a great light.
Shep'd 1	And in the light were angels.
Shep'd 2	The angels spoke to us, sir!
Shep'd 3	They said—Go to Bethlehem, and worship the child you shall find there.
Shep'd 1	And then the angels sang, they sang all together.
Shep'd 2	Glory to God in the highest—that is what they sang, sirs, in the middle of all that bright light.
Shep'd 3	We were frightened, sirs. Have you, too, seen the angels?
1st King	We have seen visions.
2nd King	We have heard voices.
3rd King	We have seen the light of the star.
1st King	And now the star has stopped.
2nd King	It is over our heads.
3rd King	This is the place.

(They all look around)

1st King	This? This is nothing but the cowshed of an inn!
Shep'd 1	You shall find him in a manger! You shall find the child in a manger. That is what the angels told us.
Shep'd 2	They did! In a manger. That *is* what they said! And where would you find a manger?
Shep'd 3	In a cowshed!
1st King	Then our journey is over.
2nd King	In Bethlehem.
3rd King	By a cowshed.
Shep'd 1	Tonight there is no difference between rich kings and poor shepherds.
1st King	No difference. Tonight all men are brothers.
Shep'd 2	How strange!
2nd King	We all feel it!
Shep'd 3	We all know it.
3rd King	Then brothers, let us all go in and see this king.

(They all exit together, centre, through the curtains. The Roman Officer comes onto the forestage from the side)

Officer	So this is where they expect to find their king! In a cowshed! But what can you expect from old men and foolish shepherds? Voices and angels, visions and stars, indeed! But duty is duty, a job is a job— I'd better have a look for myself.

(As he starts to follow through the centre of the curtains they open to reveal the Nativity tableau on the full stage. The officer stares at the scene for a moment. Then he, too, slowly goes down on his knees. Offstage the choir sings a carol softly.
During this, the Kings and Shepherds present their gifts. Then they move forward to the forestage, followed by the Officer, while the curtains slowly close)

Kings	We have seen the king!
Shep'ds	We have heard angels speaking the words of the prophets!
Officer	Praise the name of this new king!
1st King	*You* say that?
Officer	I have seen him.
Shep'd 1	Do *you* believe he is the king?
Officer	I have seen him. I believe.
2nd King	We must take this news to King Herod.
Officer	No—you must not! Herod wishes to slay this king.
3rd King	Must we disobey Herod?
Shep'ds	You must, sirs! Herod must never know.
Officer	Go home another way, my brothers. Travel through deserts and mountains, but do not go where Herod may find you. Go, sirs, go!
1st King	And you? What of you?
Shep'ds	Yes, what of you?
Officer	Go! Go! Keep this secret in your hearts until it is safe to tell it. The time will come.
All	But what of you?
Officer	I shall pray, my brothers, and I shall stay to serve this Lord and King.

(The curtains of the full stage open once more on the Nativity tableau. All slowly kneel, the Roman Officer in the centre with his back to the audience. As the choir softly hums a carol he raises his bowed head, draws his sword and lifts it above his head with both hands. Then he slowly lowers it and places it with the other gifts. As he bows his head once more the humming of the choir swells and the curtains slowly close)

The First Nowell would be a suitable carol to use. Sing the first five verses while the gifts are being presented. At the end, hum the tune softly and then sing the last verse louder as the curtains close.

Index

Answers

Page 19 What Did Santa Claus Bring?
puppet, kite, skateboard, watch, toy rabbit, locomotive, sled, ball, scarf, hat, recorder (instrument), candy, party snapper, jar of candy.

Page 38 Pantomime Puzzle
E=1 ALADDIN AND HIS MAGIC LAMP
B=2 SLEEPING BEAUTY
G=3 JACK AND THE BEANSTALK
A=4 WOLF FROM LITTLE RED RIDING HOOD
D=5 UGLY SISTERS FROM CINDERELLA
C=6 PUSS-IN-BOOTS
F=7 HUMPTY-DUMPTY

Page 43 Pass the Parcel
A puppet